Nebraska Intellectual Freedom Manual

Round Table on Intellectual Freedom
Nebraska Library Association

Zea Books / University of Nebraska-Lincoln Libraries 2016

Nebraska Library Association Intellectual Freedom Manual

2016 edition

Editors

Michael Elsener and Sue Ann Gardner

Contributors

K. Joan Birnie	Broken Bow Public Library, Broken Bow, Nebraska
Karen Drevo	Norfolk Public Library, Norfolk, Nebraska
Brenda Ealey	Lincoln City Libraries, Lincoln, Nebraska
Michael Elsener	Southeast Community College, Lincoln, Nebraska
Sue Ann Gardner	University of Nebraska-Lincoln, Lincoln, Nebraska
Timothy Lentz	University of Nebraska-Lincoln, Lincoln, Nebraska
Todd Schlechte	Southeast Library System, Lincoln, Nebraska

UNIVERSITY OF Nebraska Lincoln®

Imprint: Published for Intellectual Freedom, a round table of the Nebraska Library Association, by Zea Books, an imprint of the University of Nebraska-Lincoln Libraries.

ISBN: 978-1-60962-093-6

Table of Contents

I: Introduction

Much has changed in libraries and society since the publication of the 2004 revision of the Nebraska Library Association *Intellectual Freedom Manual*. The consensus of the current members of the Nebraska Library Association round table on Intellectual Freedom (NLA IF) was not to just revise the former manual, but to create an entirely new edition. In doing so, the authors have addressed a number of new issues. The intention was to keep it relatively brief but still useful. Readers should be able to read sections independent of one another for quick reference on topics of interest. For readers of the electronic version, there are many hyperlinks included.

Though this is a new edition, the introduction to the 2004 revision still applies:

> As librarians, we are all concerned with the concept of intellectual freedom. It is our professional obligation to provide varied forms of information that meet the varied interests and needs of our community members. It is also our professional obligation to oppose the efforts of those who would attempt to monitor, challenge, change, or remove the materials of choice in our society.
>
> This handbook provides access to relevant resources for all librarians who may face a censorship challenge. Included are interpretations from the Library Bill of Rights, policies and procedures, examples of useful forms, and a list of library related organizations that may be contacted for further information.

For additional information, readers are encouraged to consult the latest edition of the American Library Association (ALA) *Intellectual Freedom Manual*, as well as manuals from other U.S. states' library organizations. A companion to the ALA manual is available online at http://www.ifmanual.org/. For current information about intellectual freedom issues in Nebraska, visit the NLA IF website.

II: Library Ethics

As is stated on the American Library Association (ALA) library ethics website, librarians and library staff "significantly influence or control the selection, organization, preservation, and dissemination of information. In a political system grounded in an informed citizenry, we are members of a profession explicitly committed to intellectual freedom and the freedom of access to information. We have a special obligation to ensure the free flow of information and ideas to present and future generations."

The ALA Code of Ethics should be recognized by Nebraska librarians, library staff, boards, volunteers, users, and advocates as key to the services libraries provide. The Code speaks to relationships with library customers and colleagues. It outlines areas critical to the library profession and to the qualities that make libraries unique and vital in the communities served.

Ethics in the library, like those in other spheres of life, should not be taken lightly or applied arbitrarily. Ethics are not intended to be easy—they raise the bar and challenge us to perform at our best. Ethical conduct strengthens the library profession and expedites attainment of shared goals.

III: Intellectual Freedom Explained

As defined by the American Library Association (ALA), intellectual freedom is "the right of every individual to both seek and receive information from all points of view without restriction. It provides for free access to all expressions of ideas through which any and all sides of a question, cause, or movement may be explored."

Intellectual freedom is a tenet that makes the library profession unique, in serving the minority as well as the majority—in collections that reflect the unpopular as well as the popular—and in protecting the utmost privacy of library users. Intellectual freedom cannot be limited or extended by personal beliefs and preferences. Intellectual freedom is a foundational principle that encourages tolerance and diversity.

Intellectual freedom is a challenging area of discussion which lends itself to increasingly complicated concerns. These issues often involve law and court decisions, so they can be affected by changing decisions and ongoing appeals and suits.

Following is additional information about various relevant topics and concerns of interest to Nebraska librarians and patrons.

IV: Freedom of Speech

Central to intellectual freedom is the freedom of speech, the right to speak out publicly or privately. The term covers all forms of expression, including books, newspapers, magazines, radio, television, motion pictures, technology, and the internet. As covered in foundational documents, such as the U.S. Constitution and subsequent U.S. Supreme Court decisions, there are areas of speech that receive no protection or limited protection, such as: commercial speech, obscenity[1], fighting words, child pornography, defamation, and troop location at a time of war.

In public areas of the library, such as on bulletin boards, in meeting rooms, in exhibits, and distributed literature, library staff cannot discriminately select materials based on the content of speech or expression, or refuse to provide access to patrons based solely on the viewpoint expressed. Limitations may be placed on the time, place, or manner of access to library resources, but these choices must reflect a neutral viewpoint and be by the least restrictive means. If the intent of a challenger is removal of an expression because of disagreement with the content, it is unconstitutional[2].

V: Unrestricted Access to Resources

Libraries promote an open exchange of information and the right to freedom of expression in a public space as guaranteed by the First Amendment to the United States Constitution. ALA's Code of Ethics and Library Bill of Rights dictate the guiding principles of intellectual freedom for all library users. These principles allow patrons of the library unrestricted and equal access to all resources in all formats, including print, digital, sound, visual, and electronic media, regardless of the patron's origin, background, disability, age, viewpoints, reading level, economic status, housing status, veteran status, gender identity, gender expression, or sexual orientation.

---

[1] Pornography is not illegal, unless it involves children. Just because something is sexually explicit does not mean it is obscene—that's a decision made by the courts and the work must be considered as a whole.

[2] Board of Education v. Pico, 457 U.S. 853 (1982) and Case v. Unified School Dist., 908 F. Supp. 864 (D. Kan. 1995).

Libraries must facilitate access in every way possible. This means reading, listening, and viewing are individual, private matters. While anyone is free to select or reject materials for themselves or their own minor children, the freedom of others to read or inquire will not be restricted. Library materials are not restricted, sequestered, altered, or labeled by the library because of controversy about the author or the subject matter. Library actions and decisions made in order to avoid controversy often invite trouble.

Due to limited space and resources, a library cannot make all materials available. If the library does not have material that reflects a patron's viewpoint, that patron should be able to speak with a staff librarian about the issue. The library's collection, no matter the format of the material, should not restrict controversial material and should reflect a variety of perspectives and viewpoints. A system for ordering or borrowing items through interlibrary loan should be in place.

Libraries should have a policy and guidelines regarding formal requests to challenged resources. Policies must always protect the confidentiality of library users and their records. See the section on guidelines for creating policies to respond to challenges.

Library services should be available at no cost to patrons, if possible. If they cannot be provided for free, measures should be taken to minimize any barriers to the public to obtain information. Users should have access to open and unfiltered internet content. Library meeting rooms should be available to the public, and not be restricted based on the popularity of viewpoints presented.

In general, librarians are guided by a commitment to provide wide access to information. They should be guided by the ALA statements on access to information, namely, the Library Bill of Rights and Interpretations of the Library Bill of Rights, Freedom to Read Statement, and ALA Code of Ethics. They must work to enact policies that provide appropriate protections to their patrons while being consistent with the principles of free expression as set forth in the First Amendment to the United States Constitution.

VI: Internet Filtering and Intellectual Freedom

Librarians are consistent champions of intellectual freedom, but community values and state and federal laws can come into conflict around the issue of offensive or unwelcome internet content. Filtering is generally anathema to intellectual freedom, and by extension, librarianship as a profession. Given this conflict in values, it is crucial for librarians to be well-informed and to be prepared to address intellectual freedom with respect to internet access and content filtering of websites. These conversations could involve patrons, governing boards, community groups, and government agencies, and good preparation can ease these potentially difficult or challenging discussions.

Despite the commonplace use of filtering software, the effectiveness of filters is still an open question. Internet users can gain access to content, legal or otherwise, in ways that simply can't be stopped by filtering. Nonetheless, for financial reasons or because of strong community feelings around the internet's potential for delivering uncomfortable material (whether or not such material is constitutionally protected), many librarians do employ filters. With or without filtering, though, good preparation in terms of staff training and knowledge, clear policy, and good communication with community stakeholders is crucial.

At this time, Nebraska has no laws governing internet access beyond existing federal legislation, so the issue is simplified in Nebraska libraries. Whether filtering software is or is not employed, some important issues must be considered.

A: E-Rate and the Children's Internet Protection Act

Libraries that receive federal funding through e-rate discounts[3] on internet service or the Library Services and Technology Act (LSTA) must comply with the Children's Internet Protection Act (CIPA). Content filtering is required by CIPA, as is the establishment of a governing policy for internet use. However, if libraries choose to forgo federal funds, they are not required to implement filtering.

If federal monies are refused with the intent to avoid filters, it may be useful to set up other arrangements, such as privacy screens, youth and adult labs, and very clear guidelines about parental responsibility for any content retrieved online. Nonetheless, libraries exist within the context of the communities they serve, and while legal details are very important, it is equally necessary to recognize and work within the values of the surrounding community.

B: Filtering Software Considerations

If filtering protocols are used, strive to choose the best software available. It should be viewpoint-neutral, and should allow the ability to be switched off or customized as needed to allow content that is legal under the First Amendment. Once the software is chosen, take the time to maintain and monitor the software effectively.

If the institution already has filtering software in place, take the time to run a cost-benefit analysis. The costs of purchasing software, maintaining that software, training staff to deal effectively with blocking or unblocking web pages, taken all together, may outweigh the savings of federal discounts or funding.

VII: Intellectual Freedom for Minors

Young people have First Amendment rights. Librarians and governing bodies should maintain that parents or legal guardians—and only parents or legal guardians—have the right and the responsibility to restrict the access to library resources for their children—and only their children. Censorship by librarians of constitutionally protected speech, whether for the supposed protection of children, or for any other reason, violates the First Amendment. Librarians cannot restrict access to information for minors or censor material to protect children from controversial viewpoints.

Many video games and movies have ratings on the packaging. These ratings are not legally binding and should not determine whether a minor can check out these resources. Furthermore, required parental permission forms are unadvisable since they create a stigma and present a barrier to access. Patrons and staff should not have any illusion that they can sanitize a youth collection or section. This is essentially a straightforward concept but there may be challenges due to perceived nuances. For example,

[3] See the Nebraska Library Commission website for more information about e-rate in Nebraska, http://nlc.nebraska.gov/erate/.

school librarians may operate *in loco parentis* in providing the physical well-being of a minor or safe from harm as their parents or legal guardians would.

VIII: Intellectual Freedom for Authors: A Very Brief Overview of United States Copyright[4]

A: What Can Be Copyrighted and What Rights Are Conferred?

In the United States, copyright applies to an original work (a text, sound recording, art work, or one of several other forms) once it has been fixed in a tangible form (this would be a manuscript, in the case of textual works). Ideas and processes cannot be copyrighted.

Copyright entitles the holder exclusively to exercise the right to:

1.   Make copies of the work
2.   Create derivative works
3.   Distribute the work
4.   Perform or display the work.

Exclusive in this case means that no one else has the right to do these things legally, except when given permission by the rights holder or under the terms of Fair Use (see below).

B: Who Owns Copyright in a Work?

Copyright is held, at least initially, by the creator of a work, unless the work was made for hire, meaning, in the course of the creator's job. Some employers, like universities, often have policies that reconfer copyright back to the creator of a work developed in the course of employment, usually with some exceptions. Works created by United States government employees in the course of their jobs are in the public domain, meaning, not copyrighted.

A work created by joint authors is copyrighted by all authors equally, so each author can make unilateral decisions about what to do with the work. It is commonly asserted that if an article is written by several authors, the article exists as a unified entity and copyright covers it in its entirety. Parts of it are not copyrighted separately, unless there is a clearly distinguished portion, such as a graphic element that could stand on its own.

There is no age requirement for an author for a work to be copyrighted. Works by children are copyrighted by them, not their parents or caretakers.

C: Copyright Formalities

A work does not have to be formally published and no registration is required to copyright a work, though registration with the United States Library of Congress is required in order to sue for copyright infringement. A copyright symbol is not required for a work to be considered copyrighted in the United States. As soon as a work is in a fixed, tangible form, it is copyrighted.

---

[4] No legal advice is implied. Always consult with a qualified professional in cases of legal matters.

D: **Transfer of Copyright**

Though copyright is held initially by the creator of a work, the rights can be transferred. Publishers and producers often require that copyright be transferred to them before they will edit and/or distribute a work. A creator cannot reclaim copyright once he or she has given it away, and the creator of the work can no longer legally copy, derive from, distribute, perform, or display the work, either the published version or the manuscript, unless the new copyright holder gives the creator permission to do so.

Ownership of a copyrighted item does not bring with it ownership of the copyright itself. Just as if someone owns a book, that person does not own the copyrights in the book. Or someone may possess a letter, but only the author owns the copyright in it. Photographers possess the copyright of their photographs, the subjects in the photographs do not own the rights.

E: **Length of Term of Copyright**

The length of term of copyright varies depending on several factors, but suffice it to say that it is very long—for example, the life of the author plus seventy years. The copyright term can also be formally extended in most circumstances.

F: **Permissions and Licensing**

The person or entity who owns copyright in an original work can permit others to use the work, either case-by-case or through a license. A license communicates what permissions are allowed by whom and what restrictions there are over use, such as being required to attribute the copyright holder, for instance.

Copyright holders do not have to give permissions to anyone, though some use without explicit permission would be considered fair (see below). Or a license may be imposed that effectively places the work in the public domain, such as a Creative Commons Zero (CC0) license which gives anyone the right to copy, distribute, derive, display, or perform the work with no explicit permission and no attribution required. Licenses run the gamut between those extremes.

G: **Fair Use**

In the United States, use of a work without explicit permission from the copyright holder for criticism, comment, news reporting, teaching, scholarship, or research, is not considered to be an infringement. This sort of use is legally called Fair Use. Much litigation has occurred around this concept and whether any particular use would be considered legally fair is not clear cut.

The guidelines to help a user determine whether a use may be considered to be a legally fair use consist of the following factors:

1.   Whether the use is commercial or is for nonprofit educational purposes
2.   The nature of the work
3.   The amount and substantiality of the portion used
4.   The effect on the potential market of the work.

H: Consequences of Infringement

Copyright infringement can be a civil or a criminal offense. Remedies vary, but can involve simple take down requests, or can include monetary damages and even jail time.

IX: Advocacy and Media Relations

Cultivating a relationship with the media is an avenue for making the library visible, preferably before there is a problem. Files of policies and key messages should be kept together for easy access, and staff should practice using them. Librarians and members of library boards need to build a relationship with local media proactively—including making library staff easy to find. If staff are not available, someone else may speak on their behalf.

X: Privacy and Confidentiality

A: Ethical Considerations

Preserving patron privacy is a core part of who we are as librarians. As the ALA Code of Ethics states: "We protect each library user's right to privacy and confidentiality with respect to information sought or received and resources consulted, borrowed, acquired, or transmitted." Lack of privacy dampens free inquiry and may intimidate individuals so that they will not access all resources offered by the library.

Librarians strive to provide open access to information while protecting a patron's privacy and confidentiality. Libraries afford diverse views to the public for the interest of knowledge and learning; patrons should never be judged by the material they read or the information they collect. Both privacy and confidentiality are essential to intellectual freedom.

Privacy allows users to explore information without judgment by others. Intellectual freedom is challenged when there is a risk to privacy. Confidentiality is maintained through the records a library keeps on each patron. Patrons trust that the library will allow them the privacy to explore multiple and even unpopular viewpoints without fear of repercussion. All library records must be kept confidential.

B: Legal Considerations

Libraries not only have an ethical basis for protecting privacy, but also possess a legal prerogative. The First, Fourth, Fifth, Ninth, Tenth, and first section of the Fourteenth Amendments to the United States Constitution, and portions of the Nebraska Constitution, speak to this, assuring that individuals have the right to receive information free from fear of intrusion, intimidation, or reprisal. Courts have upheld the fundamental right to privacy on the basis of the First and Fourth Amendments to the United States Constitution. Further, Nebraska State Statute guarantees the right of libraries to formulate policy which protects the privacy of library users:

> The following records, unless publicly disclosed in an open court, open
> administrative proceeding, or open meeting or disclosed by a public entity

pursuant to its duties, may be withheld from the public by the lawful custodian of the records... (11) Records or portions of records kept by a publicly funded library which, when examined with or without other records, reveal the identity of any library patron using the library's materials or services...[5]

As detailed in the section in this manual on responding to requests from law enforcement officials, library records should not be released without presentation of legal documents, such as a subpoena or a search warrant. This is important because evidence unlawfully seized cannot be used in an investigation.

C: Issues Related to Third Party Vendors

In negotiations with third party vendors, every effort should be made to maintain patron privacy[6]. If a third party vendor makes information available about patrons, the service offered by the vendor should be optional for library users, and it should be clearly stated to what extent library users are giving up privacy when they use a library service provided by a third party. For example, some online public access catalog interfaces allow patrons to see their reading history, rate books, write book reviews, and share this information online. These should be opt in features, not opt out, so that patrons will retain complete privacy unless they choose otherwise.

D: Ensuring Privacy and Confidentiality for Library Users[7]

The Deputy Director of the ALA Office for Intellectual Freedom, Deborah Caldwell-Stone, has enumerated steps to ensuring privacy and confidentiality in the library. With permission, included here is a truncated list she has created listing some elements of privacy in the library:

1.   Observation

     a.   Even though libraries are public places, libraries, and those who work for libraries, should strive to protect users' privacy when they are using library resources, whether print or online

     b.   Carrels, stacks, and computer stations should be arranged in a manner that discourages or prevents someone reading over a user's shoulder without the user being aware of the activity

     c.   Reference desks should be arranged so that a user can ask a question in confidence without being overheard

     d.   Libraries that use surveillance cameras should have written policies stating that the cameras are not to be used for any other purpose than security

          1.   Avoid placing cameras in a manner that records what users are reading, viewing, or checking out

---

[5] Nebraska Revised Statute 84-712.05.
[6] See the NISO Privacy Principles document (2015) for detailed information about privacy issues that arise when contracting with third party vendors, available at http://www.niso.org/apps/group_public/download.php/16064/NISO%20Privacy%20Principles.pdf.
[7] Deborah Caldwell-Stone (2016), excerpt from "Privacy in Your Library: Law, Ethics, and Policy," presented at the 2016 Public Library Association Conference, Denver, Colorado, available at https://s4a.goeshow.com/temp/handouts/E504C6EB-3B8D-E411-B196-0025B3A62EEE/PLAChangingLandscapeofPrivacyDocs.pdf, reprinted with permission.

2.   If the cameras create records via film, tape, or electronic files, the library must recognize its responsibility to protect the confidentiality of those records like any other library record, including purging the records as soon as their purpose is served.

2.   Anonymity

     a.   "The right to open inquiry without having the subject of one's interest examined or scrutinized by others" includes the ability to use library resources anonymously

     b.   Anonymity is an important factor in providing equity of access to information, particularly for those who are members of especially vulnerable groups

     c.   Where possible and feasible, allow the use of pseudonyms, aliases, guest log-ins, anonymizing software and community terminals for those who request them

     d.   Where anonymity is not possible, provide information about the library's commitment to confidentiality.

Caldwell-Stone has also identified some fundamental privacy procedures in the library[8]. The list is included here, with permission:

1.   Avoid creating unnecessary records
2.   Avoid retaining records that are not needed for efficient operation of the library, including data-related logs, digital records, vendor-collected data, and system backups
3.   Limit the degree to which personally identifiable information is monitored, collected, disclosed, and distributed
4.   Avoid library practices and procedures that place personally identifiable information on public view
5.   Employ robust encryption and cybersecurity measures to protect user data. Store user data on servers in the library or, if using cloud-based services, maintain robust passwords.
6.   When user data is provided to, or managed by, a vendor providing e-content, cataloging, and data management services to the library, the library should require the vendor to enter into a legal agreement with the library that stipulates that the library retains control of its users' data, that the data is confidential, and that it may not be used or shared with third parties except with the permission of the library
7.   Key Concept: Libraries should minimize the collection of personally identifiable user information, store it locally and securely, maintain legal control of the data and insure that library practices do not divulge user information or put it on public view (e.g., self-service hold shelves that reveal a user's identity).

XI: Intellectual Freedom Policies

Policy is key. It is the foundation of library services. It should be enforced consistently and be viewpoint neutral. Policies must be written with a means of appeal and applied equally. In creating and reviewing policies ask, "What about intellectual freedom might be an issue?" Key to success is a balance between individual rights and responsibilities. There is no right to not be offended.

---

[8] Deborah Caldwell-Stone (2016), excerpt from "Privacy in Your Library: Law, Ethics, and Policy," presented at the 2016 Public Library Association Conference, Denver, Colorado, available at https://s4a.goeshow.com/temp/handouts/E504C6EB-3B8D-E411-B196-0025B3A62EEE/PLAChangingLandscapeofPrivacyDocs.pdf, reprinted with permission.

A: Guidelines for Policy Development

The American Library Association's Intellectual Freedom Committee has adopted Guidelines for the Development and Implementation of Policies, Regulations; and Procedures Affecting Access to Library Resources, Services, and Facilities. The Nebraska Library Association's Intellectual Freedom round table recommends that libraries follow these guidelines as they develop policy.

B: Collection Development and Resource Reconsideration

It is essential that every library develop an official collection development policy which supports the library's mission and philosophy statement, defines the purpose and scope of the collection, and guides collections work throughout the library. The policy then should be officially approved by the governing board of the library. Once adopted, the policy should be reviewed periodically and revised as necessary.

The collection development policy defines the scope, range, and focus of a library's collections and clearly states the principles and expectations for collection evaluation and maintenance, procedures for materials selection, and methodology for handling both suggestions and complaints. The policy should be distributed to library staff and made available to the public. The collection development policy should:

1.   Include the library's mission statement
2.   Clearly define the philosophy used in the selection and evaluation of materials
3.   Set forth the dimensions and limits of the library's collections
4.   Provide a written framework for planning, building, selecting, and maintaining the library's various collections
5.   List criteria used for selection and evaluation of materials
6.   Set forth a clearly defined procedure for handling resource reconsideration requests as well as suggestions from library users regarding purchase of materials
7.   Include a policy for accepting and disposing of gift materials
8.   Include clearly stated principles for collection evaluation and maintenance
9.   Include a plan for periodic review and revision
10.   Contain an appendix that contains the basics of libraries and intellectual freedom which includes links to the ALA Code of Ethics, Library Bill of Rights, Freedom to Read Statement, Libraries: An American Value, Notable First Amendment Cases, and Nebraska Laws Pertaining to Libraries and Library Operations (Statutes).

Numerous examples of well-written collection development and resource reconsideration policies are available online for review and collection development tools are available from ALA at http://www.ala.org/tools/atoz/Collection%20Development/collectiondevelopment.

C: Privacy and Confidentiality

Until a privacy and confidentiality policy is enacted in a library, the privacy of patron records is not automatically protected by law. Therefore, it is extremely important that all publicly funded libraries create such policy. It is highly advised, due to the ethical and constitutional imperative to protect privacy, that non-publicly funded libraries also carefully formulate such a policy.

Specifically with regard to records management policy, Deborah Caldwell-Stone suggests the following, included here with permission[9]:

1.   Personally identifiable information should be regularly purged, including personally identifiable information associated with library resource use, material circulation history, and security/surveillance tapes and logs
2.   "Purging" does not imply wholesale destruction of records. Statistical information, library usage data permanently stripped of personally identifiable information, and historical documents can and should be retained to aid library administration and preservation of the historical record
3.   Policies addressing records management, including purging, must be employed throughout the institution, including information technology departments and off-site locations
4.   Physical records containing users' personally identifiable information or financial information should be secured and kept from public view while needed and shredded when no longer needed.

Additional considerations when creating privacy policies:

1.   Outline how the library limits the collection of personally identifiable information
2.   Declare that circulation records and other records identifying the names of library users are confidential
3.   Explain that the library deletes information when it is no longer needed
4.   Mention that personal information will not be placed in public view, whether physically or electronically
5.   Explain that staff will refuse to divulge private information, including to law enforcement, without a subpoena or court order. See the section on visits and requests from law enforcement for more information
6.   Allow opting in to library services which give up some privacy; do not set the default as opt out.

D: Internet Use

The internet greatly expands access to knowledge and information, and nearly all libraries provide some resources for connecting to the wealth of information available online. It is essential to have a set of policies and procedures governing internet use in libraries, whether public, academic, or special libraries. Further, for libraries affected by legislation such as the Children's Internet Protection Act and the Neighborhood Children's Internet Protection Act, such policies are actually required by these laws. Always seek legal counsel for in-depth understanding of the implications of such legislation.

---

[9] Deborah Caldwell-Stone (2016), excerpt from "Privacy in Your Library: Law, Ethics, and Policy," presented at the 2016 Public Library Association Conference, Denver, Colorado, available at https://s4a.goeshow.com/temp/handouts/E504C6EB-3B8D-E411-B196-0025B3A62EEE/PLAChangingLandscapeofPrivacyDocs.pdf, reprinted with permission.

A well-rounded policy statement will be clearly posted and readily available, clearly explain steps for follow up or appeals to any part of the policy statement, and state and uphold that the policy will be implemented fairly and consistently for all patrons. A good policy should lay out the philosophical and conceptual underpinnings and should plainly state the rules that govern internet use in the library. Within the context of the rules, the policy should clearly identify the general procedures that govern the rules.

The following checklist, drawn from a similar list created by ALA, provides a quick sketch or template for creating or reviewing library policies on internet usage.

A properly written policy should:

1. Clearly state the purpose of the policy
2. Provide a brief summary of the mission and principles of the library, and how the larger mission is specifically connected to the library's internet policy
3. Offer links or references to documents such as the United States Bill of Rights, the ALA Freedom to Read statement, and the Library Bill of Rights for further context
4. Identify users' rights and responsibilities to follow the law
5. Briefly discuss legally prohibited uses such as expressions of obscenity, child pornography, and any uses harmful to minors
6. Plainly state whether the library staff are or are not legally *in loco parentis*. If not, parents or legal guardians are responsible for the online content their children access
7. Explain that libraries are not legally responsible for any content available online, even content that falls outside the bounds of the prohibitions discussed above
8. Provide a brief explanation of any filtering software, and the policy for requesting the removal of filtering or unblocking of permissible content
9. Discuss how the library protects the confidentiality and privacy of its patrons online.

The procedures that govern the policy should:

1. Explain the consequences of failure to observe the rules, legal or otherwise
2. Include basic information, such as computer reservations and time limits
3. Identify specific procedures connected to the rules around unblocking content or removing filtering.

E: Internet Filtering

Good policies regarding the use of filtering are essential to safeguard the institution against liability. Consult with legal counsel, and with colleagues at state and local library agencies, to create solid guidelines around internet use in the library. A clear statement that the library is not legally liable for content published and accessed online serves as protection from legal action if someone does something illegal online in the library.

The policy should be written to account for liability issues around what content is accessed on unfiltered library computers, but there are also serious issues when filters act to block content that should be accessible to patrons. To avoid the possibility of litigation, and whether filtering is required or chosen optionally, a clear path should be made for patrons to get access to accidentally blocked legal content.

F: **Expected Library User Behavior**

The behavior of patrons in libraries occasionally can negatively affect the free inquiry of others. ALA's Intellectual Freedom Committee recommends that publicly supported libraries use the following guidelines, based upon constitutional principles, to develop policies and procedures governing the use of library facilities[10]:

1.   Libraries are advised to rely upon existing legislation and law enforcement mechanisms as the primary means of controlling behavior that involves public safety, criminal behavior, or other issues covered by existing local, state, or federal statutes. In many instances, this legal framework may be sufficient to provide the library with the necessary tools to maintain order

2.   If the library's governing body chooses to write its own policies and procedures regarding user behavior or access to library facilities, services, and resources, the policies should cite statutes or ordinances upon which the authority to make those policies is based

3.   Library policies and procedures governing the use of library facilities should be carefully examined to ensure that they embody the principles expressed in the Library Bill of Rights

4.   It is acceptable to create reasonable and narrowly drawn policies and procedures designed to prohibit interference with use of the facilities and services by others, or to prohibit activities inconsistent with achievement of the library's mission statement and objectives

5.   Locally crafted policies and the attendant implementing procedures should be reviewed frequently by the library's legal counsel for compliance with federal and state constitutional requirements, federal and state civil rights legislation, all other applicable federal and state legislation, and applicable case law. Policies should be updated as needed

6.   Use common sense, reason, and sensitivity, to reduce the chance of escalation. Every effort should be made to respond to inappropriate user behavior in a timely, direct, and open manner

7.   Libraries should develop an ongoing staff training program based upon their user behavior policy. This program should include training to develop empathy and understanding of the social and economic problems of some library users

8.   Policies and regulations that impose restrictions on library access should:

   a.   Apply only to activities that materially interfere with the public's right of access to library facilities, the safety of users and staff, and the protection of library resources and facilities

   b.   Narrowly tailor prohibitions or restrictions so that they are not more restrictive than needed to serve their objectives

---

[10] Adopted by the American Library Association Intellectual Freedom Committee, January 24, 1993; revised November 17, 2000; revised January 19, 2005.

c.   Attempt to balance competing interests and avoid favoring the majority at the expense of individual rights, while not allowing individual users' rights to supersede those of the majority of library users

d.   Be based on behavior and not on arbitrary distinctions between individuals or classes of individuals. Policies should not target specific users or groups of users based on an assumption or expectation that such users might engage in behaviors that could disrupt library service

e.   Not restrict access to the library by persons who merely inspire the anger or annoyance of others. Policies based upon appearance or behavior that is merely annoying or that merely generates negative subjective reactions from others, do not meet the necessary standard. Such policies should employ a reasonable, objective standard based on the behavior itself

f.   Provide a clear description of behavior that is prohibited and the various enforcement measures in place so that patrons will have both due process and fair warning. This description must be continuously and clearly communicated to library users

g.   Not leave those affected without adequate alternative means of access to information in the library, as much as possible

h.   Be enforced evenhandedly, and not in a manner intended to benefit or disfavor any person or group in an arbitrary or capricious manner.

The user behaviors addressed in these guidelines are the result of a wide variety of individual and societal conditions. Libraries should take advantage of the expertise of local social service agencies, advocacy groups, mental health professionals, law enforcement officials, and other community resources to develop strategies for addressing the needs of a diverse population.

G: Use of Meeting Rooms and Exhibit Spaces

If a publicly funded library has a meeting room, exhibit space, or display space, then it needs a policy that addresses the use of that space. If it limits meeting rooms to library programs (for example, because the library holds a very large number of events in the room) and exhibits only staff-selected displays, then the policy may be very short but should still exist.

The first part of the policy should explain how the use of the meeting room is linked with the library's mission. The purpose of the room needs to be clearly stated. The policy should further describe the meeting room in detail and define who is eligible to use the meeting room.

A publicly funded library may never restrict use of its meeting room based on the content of the meeting. For example, although some have argued that religious services should be excluded on the basis of the establishment clause of the First Amendment, this is actually a content-based restriction. Legal cases concerning defense of restrictions on religious worship in library meeting rooms have consistently been lost. Not only must rules be content-neutral, they must be applied equally to all groups who apply for use, and be narrowly defined in regard to time, place, or manner of use.

Examples of reasonable restrictions are the number of people allowed in the room (fire code), maintaining noise at a level such that it is not heard in the main part of the library (if the meeting room is not sound-proofed), limits on the number of times per month that a group may use a room, and the prohibition of the collection of money. It is also acceptable to state that library programs preempt all other activities. Other conditions may require that a representative of the group requesting to use the room must be a library card holder, or that only non-profit groups may use the room. Commercial groups may be charged a fee. A public library may require groups to allow anyone to attend as long as those persons are not disruptive, as this is consistent with the library's mission to serve the entire community.

Libraries that don't receive public funding have more discretion, but they should still try to open up access as much as possible if they allow groups to meet in their spaces. This is in accordance with the Library Bill of Rights.

When creating policies, a good question to ask is "How would the library defend itself if sued?" Consistently basing meeting room decisions on a clearly stated policy that contains narrow restrictions will provide a solid foundation. If ever faced with a lawsuit because an application was denied, the court will examine not only the policy, but the consistency with which the policy has been applied.

Finally, it is also wise to provide for an appeals process for those who have had applications denied.

H: Labeling and Rating of Materials

The ALA Library Bill of Rights covers the issue of unintended censorship that is imposed in the form of affixing warning labels to materials or assigning ratings to items. Users may be invited to self-select and rate materials via an online catalog or to list several favorites in a particular genre, for example, but the library staff should remain neutral with respect to the value of any given item. See information on the ALA website about remaining viewpoint neutral and avoiding labeling and rating systems.

XII: Response Strategies

A: Response Strategies to Attempts at Censorship

According to the American Library Association (ALA), "A challenge is an attempt to remove or restrict materials, based upon the objections of a person or group. Challenges do not simply involve a person expressing a point of view; rather, they are an attempt to remove material from the curriculum or library, thereby restricting the access of others."[11]
The ALA's Office of Intellectual Freedom offers excellent guidelines on how to respond to challenges, especially with regard to communicating effectively, kids and libraries, and school libraries.

Here are a few general tips when responding to challenges:

1.   Listen, smile, be open and positive, and try to stay calm

---

[11] Quote from American Library Association, Office for Intellectual Freedom, http://www.ala.org/bbooks/challengedmaterials.

2. Avoid being overly apologetic, defensive, or giving a mini-lesson on intellectual freedom
3. Thank the patron for sharing his or her concern
4. Provide information about your library's selection policy
5. Provide information about the Freedom to Read statement, Library Bill of Rights, and any interpretations that relate to his or her particular concern
6. Provide information about your library's reconsideration procedures
7. If the patron is not satisfied and wants to continue to pursue the challenge, provide him or her with a reconsideration form
8. Inform your supervisor, manager, or director of the incident so the school/library can be prepared if they have to deal with any further actions of the concerned patron, the public, or media.

See the list of organizations provided in section XIII for further assistance when responding to challenges.

B: **Response Strategies to Visits and Requests from Law Enforcement**

A visit from law enforcement should not alter the bond between the public and their library. Librarians must understand their rights and responsibilities when confronted by law enforcement and should have a policy in place to handle any inquiries that will protect the public's interest.

1. **Meeting with a Law Enforcement Officer**

One person should be designated to be the contact for law enforcement. Whenever possible, this should be the library director. There should be a written policy regarding confidentiality. All staff, including volunteers, should be trained to understand legal policies related to the library.

When a law enforcement officer approaches the front line staff, the librarian should ask for identification, and then direct the officer to the appropriate contact person. Staff should always document every interaction with law enforcement personnel.

If any library staff person suspects criminal activity has taken place in the library, he or she should consult with the library director and contact local authorities. Always make sure law enforcement personnel have obtained a proper court order before releasing any confidential information and notify the library's legal counsel as soon as possible.

2. **If a Law Enforcement Officer Requests Assistance without a Warrant**

Explain to law enforcement personnel that due to the privacy policies of the library, library staff will comply with requests only with a proper judicial order. Not only does this reduce liability, but the case could be harmed if information is not obtained legally. If an officer claims it is an emergency and seizes library records, do not obstruct the search. To reduce the likelihood of liability, do not grant permission to law enforcement personnel. Keep detailed records of the incident to provide documentation to the library's legal counsel.

3.   If a Law Enforcement Officer Issues a Search Warrant

A search warrant allows an officer to take immediate action, though staff can attempt to delay the search until legal counsel can examine the warrant. If law enforcement personnel insist on proceeding immediately, examine the search warrant to determine if it is current and was issued by a court in the state of Nebraska. When complying with a warrant or subpoena, follow the orders strictly and do not provide any additional information. Record the items seized from the library and ask the officer to sign a receipt detailing the inventory. If the search warrant is valid, assist the officer and keep detailed records of the incident.

4.   If a Law Enforcement Officer Issues a Subpoena

Remember that a subpoena does not require an immediate response. Refer the subpoena to legal counsel. The lawyers will advise about defects in the subpoena and may request that it be corrected before any action is taken. Repeat this process with an updated subpoena. The subpoena should be strictly limited in the scope of information granted.

5.   Actions Taken as a Result of the USA PATRIOT Act

The Uniting and Strengthening America by Providing Appropriate Tools Required to Intercept and Obstruct Terrorism (USA PATRIOT) Act was passed following the terrorist attacks on September 11, 2001. The PATRIOT Act expanded the powers of the federal government to allow access to library records through the secret legal proceedings of the Foreign Intelligence Surveillance Act (FISA) court, bypassing the traditional court system. Section 215 of the PATRIOT Act allows Federal agents to obtain library records.

If an agent from the United States Federal Bureau of Investigation presents an order subject to a nondisclosure or gag order related to the USA PATRIOT Act, examine the order to determine the time in which items must be handed over. If it is immediate, proceed as if it is a search warrant. The gag order forbids disclosing the order was received. The librarian does have the right to notify the library director and legal counsel.

XIII: Where to Get Help and Become Involved

Challenges to freedom of thought and to privacy will occur occasionally in many Nebraska libraries. Exceptions may exist if the community is well educated on intellectual freedom issues, the library staff is adept in its communication or, conversely, if the library self-censors. It is important to clearly recognize challenges to freedom of inquiry and expression, as well as to privacy. These are threats to constitutionally guaranteed freedoms. At the same time, librarians need to recognize concerns and communicate positively. It is also important to establish a network of support and to realize that not only library associations, but also other organizations, exist to offer support.

Additional information on intellectual freedom topics can be gathered from the following sources, where the name of the organization serves as a link to that organization's website.

A: **National**

1. **American Library Association, Office for Intellectual Freedom**

   The ALA's Office for Intellectual Freedom exists to educate and support librarians on issues involving intellectual freedom.

2. **American Library Association, Intellectual Freedom Round Table**

   The ALA's Intellectual Freedom Round Table:

   a.   Provides broad opportunities for ALA members to become involved in the support of freedom of access and freedom of expression in libraries

   b.   Supports librarians involved in censorship controversies

   c.   Monitors intellectual freedom developments affecting library and information services

   d.   Provides a forum where ALA members involved in intellectual freedom activities on the state and local level can discuss programs, activities, and problems

   e.   Organizes conference programs on topics related to intellectual freedom.

3. **American Library Association, Intellectual Freedom Committee**

   The ALA IFC is charged with recommending steps to safeguard the rights of library users and librarians in accordance with the First Amendment to the United States Constitution and the ALA Library Bill of Rights. With the promise of adding several more soon, they have created two sets of privacy guidelines, one with respect to ebooks and another concerning K-12 students.

4. **Electronic Frontier Foundation**

   As the name suggests, the EFF is concerned mainly with the digital world. From its website: "Founded in 1990, EFF champions user privacy, free expression, and innovation through impact litigation, policy analysis, grassroots activism, and technology development. We work to ensure that rights and freedoms are enhanced and protected as our use of technology grows."

5. **Libraries and the Internet Toolkit**

   The ALA has produced a toolkit to assist librarians in managing the internet and educating their patrons about how to use it effectively. The ALA encourages all libraries to implement policies that protect both children and public access to information, and to take an active role in educating their communities about this important resource.

6. Choose Privacy Week

Choose Privacy Week is an initiative supported by the American Library Association that invites people into a national conversation about privacy rights in a digital age. The campaign gives individuals the resources to think critically and make more informed choices about their privacy.

7. Banned Books Week Coalition

The BBWC is a national alliance of diverse organizations committed to increase awareness of the annual celebration of the freedom to read. The Coalition seeks to engage communities and inspire participation in Banned Books Week through education, advocacy, and the creation of programming about the problem of book censorship. Banned Books Week was launched in 1982 in response to a sudden surge in the number of challenges to books in schools, bookstores, and libraries. More than 11,300 books have been challenged since 1982 according to the ALA.

8. National Coalition against Censorship

The NCAC is a coalition of organizations which oppose censorship in every form. The ALA is a member. The NCAC provides a form to report censorship, maintains a blog on free expression issues, and provides resources and activities to help educate constituents. Although the NCAC is a national organization, it is willing to work on the local level, which includes helping individual libraries deal with censorship issues.

9. American Association of School Librarians, Intellectual Freedom Committee

The AASL IFC serves to protect intellectual freedom in school library programs. It communicates the difference between selection and censorship, advises about what to do before a challenge occurs and, where to obtain assistance during a challenge, and explains why schools filter and how it affects students' intellectual freedom.

10. Foundation for Individual Rights in Education

From the FIRE website, "The mission of FIRE is to defend and sustain individual rights at America's colleges and universities. These rights include freedom of speech, legal equality, due process, religious liberty, and sanctity of conscience — the essential qualities of individual liberty and dignity. FIRE's core mission is to protect the unprotected and to educate the public and communities of concerned Americans about the threats to these rights on our campuses and about the means to preserve them."

11. Great Websites for Kids

Great Websites for Kids is a compilation of exemplary websites geared to children from birth to age 14. Using established selection criteria, a committee comprising Association for Library Service to Children members evaluates suggested sites for inclusion.

B: **Nebraska and Regional**

1. **Nebraska Library Association, round table on Intellectual Freedom**

   The NLA's IF round table can connect library staff to experts in the area of intellectual freedom and help when staff face intellectual freedom issues. It also acts to spread information on intellectual freedom issues via email, blog, an updated intellectual freedom manual, spring meetings, and workshops at the NLA fall conference.

2. **Nebraska Statutes, Chapter 51, on libraries**

   Chapter 51 of the Nebraska Statutes includes formal written enactments of the Nebraska Legislature that pertain to libraries in the State.

3. **Nebraska Library Commission**

   Created to promote, develop, and coordinate library services statewide, the Nebraska Library Commission provides access to Nebraska-related information about E-Rate, the Children's Internet Protection Act, and links to filtering resources.

4. **American Civil Liberties Union of Nebraska**

   The ACLU of Nebraska has librarians on its board and approaches intellectual freedom issues the same way librarians do. The ACLU is an important ally, sometimes solving a sticky situation simply by sending a letter to a constituent about the legal issues involved. It also has attorneys on staff, which the Nebraska Library Association does not.

5. **Academic Freedom Coalition of Nebraska**

   AFCON typically operates in colleges and universities. Librarians are involved in the organization. AFCON has proved itself an important ally to librarians in Nebraska in dealing with intellectual freedom issues.

6. **Anti-Defamation League, Plains States Region**

   The Plains States Region of the Anti-Defamation League is committed to addressing the issues of prejudice and discrimination that affect the people of Nebraska, Iowa, and Kansas. To secure justice and fair treatment for all citizens, the office provides numerous educational programs to the region, monitors and exposes racial and religious extremists, and advocates for the enforcement of hate crimes legislation.

XIV: Supporting Documents, American Library Association[12]

A: ALA Library Bill of Rights[13]

The American Library Association affirms that all libraries are forums for information and ideas, and that the following basic policies should guide their services.

I.   Books and other library resources should be provided for the interest, information, and enlightenment of all people of the community the library serves. Materials should not be excluded because of the origin, background, or views of those contributing to their creation.

II.   Libraries should provide materials and information presenting all points of view on current and historical issues. Materials should not be proscribed or removed because of partisan or doctrinal disapproval.

III.   Libraries should challenge censorship in the fulfillment of their responsibility to provide information and enlightenment.

IV.   Libraries should cooperate with all persons and groups concerned with resisting abridgment of free expression and free access to ideas.

V.   A person's right to use a library should not be denied or abridged because of origin, age, background, or views.

VI.   Libraries which make exhibit spaces and meeting rooms available to the public they serve should make such facilities available on an equitable basis, regardless of the beliefs or affiliations of individuals or groups requesting their use.

---

[12] Text from the American Library Association included with permission.

[13] Adopted June 19, 1939, by the ALA Council; amended October 14, 1944; June 18, 1948; February 2, 1961; June 27, 1967; January 23, 1980; inclusion of "age" reaffirmed January 23, 1996.

B: ALA Code of Ethics[14]

As members of the American Library Association, we recognize the importance of codifying and making known to the profession and to the general public the ethical principles that guide the work of librarians, other professionals providing information services, library trustees, and library staffs.

Ethical dilemmas occur when values are in conflict. The American Library Association Code of Ethics states the values to which we are committed, and embodies the ethical responsibilities of the profession in this changing information environment.

We significantly influence or control the selection, organization, preservation, and dissemination of information. In a political system grounded in an informed citizenry, we are members of a profession explicitly committed to intellectual freedom and the freedom of access to information. We have a special obligation to ensure the free flow of information and ideas to present and future generations.

The principles of this Code are expressed in broad statements to guide ethical decision making. These statements provide a framework; they cannot and do not dictate conduct to cover particular situations.

1.   We provide the highest level of service to all library users through appropriate and usefully organized resources; equitable service policies; equitable access; and accurate, unbiased, and courteous responses to all requests.
2.   We uphold the principles of intellectual freedom and resist all efforts to censor library resources.
3.   We protect each library user's right to privacy and confidentiality with respect to information sought or received and resources consulted, borrowed, acquired or transmitted.
4.   We respect intellectual property rights and advocate balance between the interests of information users and rights holders.
5.   We treat co-workers and other colleagues with respect, fairness, and good faith, and advocate conditions of employment that safeguard the rights and welfare of all employees of our institutions.
6.   We do not advance private interests at the expense of library users, colleagues, or our employing institutions.
7.   We distinguish between our personal convictions and professional duties and do not allow our personal beliefs to interfere with fair representation of the aims of our institutions or the provision of access to their information resources.
8.   We strive for excellence in the profession by maintaining and enhancing our own knowledge and skills, by encouraging the professional development of co-workers, and by fostering the aspirations of potential members of the profession.

---

[14] Adopted at the 1939 Midwinter Meeting by the ALA Council; amended June 30, 1981; June 28, 1995; and January 22, 2008.

C: ALA Freedom to Read Statement[15]

The freedom to read is essential to our democracy. It is continuously under attack. Private groups and public authorities in various parts of the country are working to remove or limit access to reading materials, to censor content in schools, to label "controversial" views, to distribute lists of "objectionable" books or authors, and to purge libraries. These actions apparently rise from a view that our national tradition of free expression is no longer valid; that censorship and suppression are needed to counter threats to safety or national security, as well as to avoid the subversion of politics and the corruption of morals. We, as individuals devoted to reading and as librarians and publishers responsible for disseminating ideas, wish to assert the public interest in the preservation of the freedom to read.

Most attempts at suppression rest on a denial of the fundamental premise of democracy: that the ordinary individual, by exercising critical judgment, will select the good and reject the bad. We trust Americans to recognize propaganda and misinformation, and to make their own decisions about what they read and believe. We do not believe they are prepared to sacrifice their heritage of a free press in order to be "protected" against what others think may be bad for them. We believe they still favor free enterprise in ideas and expression.

These efforts at suppression are related to a larger pattern of pressures being brought against education, the press, art and images, films, broadcast media, and the internet. The problem is not only one of actual censorship. The shadow of fear cast by these pressures leads, we suspect, to an even larger voluntary curtailment of expression by those who seek to avoid controversy or unwelcome scrutiny by government officials.

Such pressure toward conformity is perhaps natural to a time of accelerated change. And yet suppression is never more dangerous than in such a time of social tension. Freedom has given the United States the elasticity to endure strain. Freedom keeps open the path of novel and creative solutions, and enables change to come by choice. Every silencing of a heresy, every enforcement of an orthodoxy, diminishes the toughness and resilience of our society and leaves it the less able to deal with controversy and difference.

Now as always in our history, reading is among our greatest freedoms. The freedom to read and write is almost the only means for making generally available ideas or manners of expression that can initially command only a small audience. The written word is the natural medium for the new idea and the untried voice from which come the original contributions to social growth. It is essential to the extended discussion that serious thought requires, and to the accumulation of knowledge and ideas into organized collections.

---

[15] This statement was originally issued in May of 1953 by the Westchester Conference of the American Library Association and the American Book Publishers Council, which in 1970 consolidated with the American Educational Publishers Institute to become the Association of American Publishers.

Adopted June 25, 1953, by the ALA Council and the AAP Freedom to Read Committee; amended January 28, 1972; January 16, 1991; July 12, 2000; June 30, 2004.

A Joint Statement by: American Library Association & Association of American Publishers. Subsequently endorsed by: American Booksellers Foundation for Free Expression, Association of American University Presses, Children's Book Council, Freedom to Read Foundation, National Association of College Stores, & National Coalition against Censorship.

We believe that free communication is essential to the preservation of a free society and a creative culture. We believe that these pressures toward conformity present the danger of limiting the range and variety of inquiry and expression on which our democracy and our culture depend. We believe that every American community must jealously guard the freedom to publish and to circulate, in order to preserve its own freedom to read. We believe that publishers and librarians have a profound responsibility to give validity to that freedom to read by making it possible for the readers to choose freely from a variety of offerings.

The freedom to read is guaranteed by the Constitution. Those with faith in free people will stand firm on these constitutional guarantees of essential rights and will exercise the responsibilities that accompany these rights.

We therefore affirm these propositions:

1. It is in the public interest for publishers and librarians to make available the widest diversity of views and expressions, including those that are unorthodox, unpopular, or considered dangerous by the majority.

2. Creative thought is by definition new, and what is new is different. The bearer of every new thought is a rebel until that idea is refined and tested. Totalitarian systems attempt to maintain themselves in power by the ruthless suppression of any concept that challenges the established orthodoxy. The power of a democratic system to adapt to change is vastly strengthened by the freedom of its citizens to choose widely from among conflicting opinions offered freely to them. To stifle every nonconformist idea at birth would mark the end of the democratic process. Furthermore, only through the constant activity of weighing and selecting can the democratic mind attain the strength demanded by times like these. We need to know not only what we believe but why we believe it.

3. Publishers, librarians, and booksellers do not need to endorse every idea or presentation they make available. It would conflict with the public interest for them to establish their own political, moral, or aesthetic views as a standard for determining what should be published or circulated.

4. Publishers and librarians serve the educational process by helping to make available knowledge and ideas required for the growth of the mind and the increase of learning. They do not foster education by imposing as mentors the patterns of their own thought. The people should have the freedom to read and consider a broader range of ideas than those that may be held by any single librarian or publisher or government or church. It is wrong that what one can read should be confined to what another thinks proper.

5. It is contrary to the public interest for publishers or librarians to bar access to writings on the basis of the personal history or political affiliations of the author.

6. No art or literature can flourish if it is to be measured by the political views or private lives of its creators. No society of free people can flourish that draws up lists of writers to whom it will not listen, whatever they may have to say.

7. There is no place in our society for efforts to coerce the taste of others, to confine adults to the reading matter deemed suitable for adolescents, or to inhibit the efforts of writers to achieve artistic expression.

8. To some, much of modern expression is shocking. But is not much of life itself shocking? We cut off literature at the source if we prevent writers from dealing with the stuff of life. Parents/legal guardians and teachers have a responsibility to prepare the young to meet

the diversity of experiences in life to which they will be exposed, as they have a responsibility to help them learn to think critically for themselves. These are affirmative responsibilities, not to be discharged simply by preventing them from reading works for which they are not yet prepared. In these matters values differ, and values cannot be legislated; nor can machinery be devised that will suit the demands of one group without limiting the freedom of others.

9. It is not in the public interest to force a reader to accept the prejudgment of a label characterizing any expression or its author as subversive or dangerous.

10. The ideal of labeling presupposes the existence of individuals or groups with wisdom to determine by authority what is good or bad for others. It presupposes that individuals must be directed in making up their minds about the ideas they examine. But Americans do not need others to do their thinking for them.

11. It is the responsibility of publishers and librarians, as guardians of the people's freedom to read, to contest encroachments upon that freedom by individuals or groups seeking to impose their own standards or tastes upon the community at large; and by the government whenever it seeks to reduce or deny public access to public information.

12. It is inevitable in the give and take of the democratic process that the political, the moral, or the aesthetic concepts of an individual or group will occasionally collide with those of another individual or group. In a free society individuals are free to determine for themselves what they wish to read, and each group is free to determine what it will recommend to its freely associated members. But no group has the right to take the law into its own hands, and to impose its own concept of politics or morality upon other members of a democratic society. Freedom is no freedom if it is accorded only to the accepted and the inoffensive. Further, democratic societies are more safe, free, and creative when the free flow of public information is not restricted by governmental prerogative or self-censorship.

13. It is the responsibility of publishers and librarians to give full meaning to the freedom to read by providing books that enrich the quality and diversity of thought and expression. By the exercise of this affirmative responsibility, they can demonstrate that the answer to a "bad" book is a good one, the answer to a "bad" idea is a good one.

14. The freedom to read is of little consequence when the reader cannot obtain matter fit for that reader's purpose. What is needed is not only the absence of restraint, but the positive provision of opportunity for the people to read the best that has been thought and said. Books are the major channel by which the intellectual inheritance is handed down, and the principal means of its testing and growth. The defense of the freedom to read requires of all publishers and librarians the utmost of their faculties, and deserves of all Americans the fullest of their support.

We state these propositions neither lightly nor as easy generalizations. We here stake out a lofty claim for the value of the written word. We do so because we believe that it is possessed of enormous variety and usefulness, worthy of cherishing and keeping free. We realize that the application of these propositions may mean the dissemination of ideas and manners of expression that are repugnant to many persons. We do not state these propositions in the comfortable belief that what people read is unimportant. We believe rather that what people read is deeply important; that ideas can be dangerous; but that the suppression of ideas is fatal to a democratic society. Freedom itself is a dangerous way of life, but it is ours.

D: **ALA Sample Request for Reconsideration of Library Resources**[16]

[This is where you identify who in your own structure, has authorized use of this form—Director, Board of Trustees, Board of Education, etc.—and to whom to return the form.]

Example: The school board of Mainstream County, U.S.A., has delegated the responsibility for selection and evaluation of library/educational resources to the school library media specialist/curriculum committee, and has established reconsideration procedures to address concerns about those resources. Completion of this form is the first step in those procedures. If you wish to request reconsideration of school or library resources, please return the completed form to the Coordinator, Media Resources, Mainstream School Dist., 1 Mainstream Plaza, Anytown, U.S.A.

Name   _____

Date   _____

Address   _____

City   _____

State   _____

Zip   _____

Phone   _____

Do you represent self? ___ Organization? ___

1. Resource on which you are commenting:
   ___ Book ___ Textbook ___ Video ___ Display ___ Magazine
   ___ Library program ___ Audio recording ___ Newspaper
   ___ Electronic information/network (please specify)
   ___ Other _____
2. Title _____
3. Author/Producer _____
4. What brought this resource to your attention?
5. Have you examined the entire resource?
6. What concerns you about the resource? (use other side or additional pages if necessary)
7. Are there resource(s) you suggest to provide additional information and/or other viewpoints on this topic?

---

[16] Revised by the American Library Association Intellectual Freedom Committee, June 27, 1995.

XV: **Supporting Documents, Pertinent Amendments to the United States Constitution**

     A: **First Amendment**

Congress shall make no law respecting an establishment of religion, or prohibiting the free exercise thereof; or abridging the freedom of speech, or of the press; or the right of the people peaceably to assemble, and to petition the government for a redress of grievances.

     B: **Fourth Amendment**

The right of the people to be secure in their persons, houses, papers, and effects, against unreasonable searches and seizures, shall not be violated, and no warrants shall issue, but upon probable cause, supported by oath or affirmation, and particularly describing the place to be searched, and the persons or things to be seized.

     C: **Fifth Amendment**

No person shall be held to answer for a capital, or otherwise infamous crime, unless on a presentment or indictment of a grand jury, except in cases arising in the land or naval forces, or in the militia, when in actual service in time of war or public danger; nor shall any person be subject for the same offense to be twice put in jeopardy of life or limb; nor shall be compelled in any criminal case to be a witness against himself, nor be deprived of life, liberty, or property, without due process of law; nor shall private property be taken for public use, without just compensation.

     D: **Ninth Amendment**

The enumeration in the Constitution, of certain rights, shall not be construed to deny or disparage others retained by the people.

     E: **Tenth Amendment**

The powers not delegated to the United States by the Constitution, nor prohibited by it to the states, are reserved to the states respectively, or to the people.

     F: **Fourteenth Amendment, Section 1**

All persons born or naturalized in the United States, and subject to the jurisdiction thereof, are citizens of the United States and of the state wherein they reside. No state shall make or enforce any law which shall abridge the privileges or immunities of citizens of the United States; nor shall any state deprive any person of life, liberty, or property, without due process of law; nor deny to any person within its jurisdiction the equal protection of the laws.